THE GOLDEN YEARS

1962

text: David Sandison, Arthur Davis

design: Paul Kurzeja

SIENA

196

Welcome to *The Golden Years*, and the kaleidoscope of world events which began to signal a change in the world order and the arrival of what would soon be known as *The Swinging Sixties*. More than any other decade, the 1960s witnessed a rush of inventions, revolutionary changes in the worlds of arts and entertainment, in human endeavour - the space race being only one example of mankind's ingenuity being matched by its courage.

This year of 1962 had more than its fair share of all those. With a new, young President entering his second year in office, the US seemed determined to forge ahead in every field, though some were proving stubbornly resistant to a sea-change in civil rights and US support for the South Vietnamese was beginning to impact on people's awareness as the cost of that support began to increase.

With the Soviet Union leading the space race, NASA began to pull out the stops and turn US know-how into US can-do, with the arrival of global television being only one of the questionable side benefits.

Justice was finally meted out to Adolf Eichmann, the war criminal hanged for his part in the Holocaust, while a severe injustice began for Nelson Mandela, jailed for the first time by the South African Government.

For much of October the world held its breath as the Cuban missile crisis unfolded on our TV screens, bringing the very real threat of World War III into our living rooms as Kennedy and Khrushchev played real-life poker with history.

We lost Marilyn, the beautiful but damaged and bewildered goddess who couldn't handle the fame and acclaim heaped on her. But we also gained The Beatles, whose first single would creep into the lower reaches of the British charts at the end of the year. None of us, including them, could guess what had been unleashed on an unsuspecting world.

It's all here, and much more besides. Have fun!

Britain Hit By Smallpox Outbreak

SIX PEOPLE WERE KNOWN TO HAVE DIED - and a further six were believed to be victims - in an outbreak of smallpox in the north of England, medical officers in Yorkshire confirmed today. One of those thought to have contracted the virus was a Leeds pathologist who'd performed an autopsy on a child casualty.

The most recent fatal victim of the disease, which had been thought to have been eradicated from Britain by child vaccination programmes, came from nearby Bradford. There, the local Medical Officer for Health announced that two more children had been admitted to hospital with suspected smallpox.

There had also been a widespread and similarly fatal outbreak of the disease in Pakistan, where 13 people were said to have died in two days.

This affected the travel plans of passengers arriving at London Airport from Holland, who were prevented from continuing their journeys after eight Pakistani immigrants complained of feeling ill on their arrival in Britain. However, it was later discovered that they were only suffering from travel sickness, but a Member of Parliament nevertheless called for vaccination against smallpox to be compulsory.

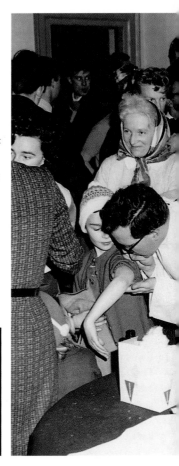

New Zealander Snell Smashes World Mile Record

The antipodean domination of the world mile record was reinforced emphatically today when a New Zealand athlete broke the record previously held by an Australian.

Peter Snell, already the reigning Olympic 800 metres champion, beat Herb Elliott's previous world record time running on a grass track at Wanganui on the North Island of New Zealand.

With Britain's Bruce Tulloh also in the field, the initial object of the race had been merely to beat the magic 'four-minute mile' barrier for the first time in New Zealand, but a blistering last lap of less than 57 seconds by Snell produced a new world record time of 3 minutes, 54.4 seconds.

US Increases Aid To Vietnam

With South Vietnam under ever-greater pressure from North Vietnamese communist guerrilla forces, President Kennedy today announced further support for the beleaguered government in the pro-Western south of the country.

In addition to military deployments already announced, the President revealed that two more US Army divisions were to be sent 'to demonstrate our determination to resist communist aggression'.

He also itemized additional financial and material aid to improve the standard of living in Vietnam, which was badly affected during World War II when it was occupied by the Japanese and, later, in the conflict with France. The new measures are expected to represent a substantial increase on the massive $130 million outlay which Kennedy authorized in 1961.

UK TOP 10 SINGLES

1: Stranger On The Shore
- Acker Bilk
2: I'll Never Find Another You
- Billy Fury
3: Let There Be Drums
- Sandy Nelson
4: The Young Ones
- Cliff Richard
5: Happy Birthday, Sweet Sixteen
- Neil Sedaka
6: Multiplication
- Bobby Darin
7: Let's Twist Again
- Chubby Checker
8: Moon River
- Danny Williams
9: Midnight In Moscow
- Kenny Ball's Jazzmen
10: Johnny Will
- Pat Boone

JANUARY 18

St Laurent Launches Fashion Empire

THE RARIFIED WORLD of *haute couture* gained a new and dynamic design house today when the French fashion sensation, Yves St Laurent, opened the doors of his own establishment in Paris with a highly acclaimed show which silenced detractors - who only two years earlier - had condemned his designs as 'fancy dress'.

After the death of his mentor, Christian Dior, in 1957, the 21-year-old St Laurent - who was born in Algeria and created his first collection in his mother's kichen - assumed control of Dior's fashion empire.

After experimenting with adventurous designs, most notably short skirts, his re-birth collection showed that St Laurent had wisely reverted to the pursuit of elegance above everything else.

Close, But No Cigar For NASA

Scientists at the NASA space centre in Florida were today trying to find out precisely what had gone wrong with their latest exercise, the attempted moon orbit of a *Ranger 3* rocket. Even by the often-vague standards of early space flight, *Ranger 3* had proved a little wayward. After straying off its pre-programmed course, NASA confirmed that it would miss the moon by more than 20,000 miles. Back to the drawing-board!

Pope Excommunicates Cuba's Castro

Cuba's socialist President, Fidel Castro, found himself at the wrong end of papal displeasure today when Vatican Radio announced that Pope John XXIII had excommunicated him from the Catholic Church.

Determined to create a socialist Utopia on his island nation, the Cuban dictator had initiated widespread social and political reforms, including the seizure and nationalization of all foreign businesses.

But it was Castro's reduction in the status of Cuba's once all-powerful clergy which proved one step too far for the Pope, and the withdrawal of Castro's right to the sacraments was his response.

De Gaulle Cracks Down On Terrorists

Confronted with a fresh wave of bombs in Paris, with politicians and journalists especially targeted, President Charles de Gaulle today ordered a nationwide increase in security to combat the French-Algerian OAS terrorists responsible. He also ordered a media block on all interviews with OAS spokesmen.

The new attacks came on the second anniversary of the first major anti-independence uprising in Algiers. The attacks were perpetrated by the OAS's self-titled Secret Army - a brigade of disgruntled French soldiers and their extreme right wing sympathizers who are intent on keeping Algeria part of France.

The OAS had already brought chaos to Algeria by successfully calling the European population out in a general strike. Among other outrages on the French mainland, it destroyed the office of the Foreign Minister, George Gorse, and kidnapped another politician, Dr Mainguy, from his surgery in the Paris suburbs. He was later freed by police after an extensive manhunt.

FEB

US Spaceman Glenn Orbits The Earth

LIEUTENANT COLONEL JOHN GLENN became the first US astronaut to orbit the earth successfully today when he spent five hours in his spacecraft before bringing it to a safe splashdown in the Atlantic, off the Puerto Rican coast.

During his historic flight, Glenn orbited the earth three times, but only after the launch of his Mercury capsule, *Friendship 7,* had been delayed five times due to problems with weather conditions at Cape Canaveral, Florida, and with computer monitoring equipment. During his first orbit, Glenn was able to recognize the city of Perth in Western Australia, where everyone had left their lights switched on!

Another unforeseen difficulty occurred shortly before *Friendship 7* was about to re-enter the earth's atmosphere, when it seemed that a protective casing had become loose. After a slight change of plan, Glenn's capsule safely parachuted into the sea, as planned.

Eight Die In Paris Protest At OAS Bombs

Street fighting in the French capital claimed eight victims today during a demonstration organized by communists protesting against recent bombings by the OAS. The dead were all crushed at the locked entrance to a Paris Metro station at the height of running battles between protesters and riot police.

However, government sources claimed that militant left-wing protesters were actually trying to undermine President de Gaulle's authority after attacks on police which resulted in over 80 casualties, some of them serious.

Even the mobilization of 25,000 armed troops in Paris failed to prevent the OAS terror campaign accelerating, with ten more bombs exploding today. They were aimed at various targets, including the author and Minister of Culture, André Malraux.

The Twist Crosses The Atlantic

The Twist - a new dance craze which swept through the US in 1961 - looked likely to do the same in Europe this month when US singer Chubby Checker's *Let's Twist Again* came close to repeating its US chart-topping feat in Britain, France and Germany.

The dance, where partners do not touch each other, was actually invented by black US singer Hank Ballard, who had a US Top 30 hit with his song in 1960. But when Chubby Checker (real name Ernest Evans) performed his version of the song on Dick Clark's *American Bandstand* TV show, and demonstrated the dance that accompanied it, teenaged America was hooked.

A second big Twist hit - *Peppermint Twist,* by Joey Dee & The Starliters - today celebrated its second week at the top of the US charts. The group are resident at New York's Peppermint Lounge, the jet-set hang-out for stars of stage and screen, the rich and the famous.

UK TOP 10 SINGLES

1: The Young Ones
- Cliff Richard
2: Let's Twist Again
- Chubby Checker
3: Rock-A-Hula-Baby
- Elvis Presley
4: Forget Me Not
- Eden Kane
5: Walk On By
- Leroy Van Dyke
6: Happy Birthday, Sweet Sixteen
- Neil Sedaka
7: Cryin' In The Rain
- The Everly Brothers
8: I'll Never Find Another You
- Eden Kane
9: Stranger On The Shore
- Acker Bilk
10: Run To Him
- Bobby Vee

Born this month:
4: Clint Black, US country music singer, songwriter
7: Garth Brooks, US country music superstar, songwriter *(see Came & Went pages)*; Axl Rose (William Bailey), US rock singer, songwriter (Guns N Roses); David Bryan, US rock musician (Bon Jovi)
8: Ken McClusky, British pop musician (The Bluebells)
15: Mike and David Milliner, British pop musicians (The Pasadenas)
16: Tony Kylie, British rock musician (Blow Monkeys)
19: Hana Mandlikova, Czech-born tennis star

Died this month:
4: Sir William Darling, Lord Provost of Edinburgh
5: Jacques Ibert, French composer
17: Bruno Walter, German-US classical conductor

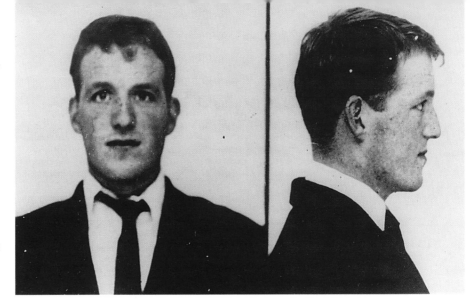

Hanratty Sentenced To Hang For A6 Murder

FEBRUARY 17

THE TRIAL OF JAMES HANRATTY, who was accused of murdering a 36-year-old man in a place ironically known as Deadman Hill, ended today with a guilty verdict and the judge pronouncing the death sentence.

It took the jury ten hours to come to their decision after hearing evidence for 21 days, which made Hanratty's the longest murder trial in British legal history. Even after hearing the verdict, Hanratty continued to protest his innocence of

the shooting, in 1961, of 36-year-old Michael Gregsten, in a lay-by on the main A6 road in Bedfordshire.

Gregsten's girlfriend, permanently paralysed by a bullet which hit her spine, identified Hanratty from the 'wide, staring

eyes' she had described to police from her bed at the Stoke Mandeville Hospital, an international centre for paraplegic injuries. Despite an appeal to the Home Secretary for clemency, Hanratty would be hanged on April 4.

U-2 Spy Plane Pilot Powers Freed In Swap

Francis Gary Powers, the US civilian pilot accused and convicted by Russia of spying in 1960, was freed today and exchanged for a leading KGB spy captured by US intelligence services.

Powers, whose U-2 aircraft was shot down over Russia after flying over top-secret military installations, had received a ten year prison sentence despite his - and the US Government's - protestations that he'd been employed to carry out metereological photography and had mistakenly strayed into Russian airspace.

Following months of top secret negotiations between the two superpowers, Powers was allowed to cross a bridge in Berlin today to reach the Western sector of the divided city, while KGB Colonel Rudolph Abel - said to be the highest ranking Russian spy ever captured by the CIA - was liberated in exchange.

US Marine Everlys Play Sullivan Show

Elvis Presley may have chosen to serve his military service as a very private soldier, but top rock duo The Everly Brothers - real-life brothers Don and Phil - did their bit for US Marine Corps recruitment in New York tonight when they appeared, in full dress uniform and regulation haircuts, on the top-rated *Ed Sullivan Show.*

The brothers, whose biggest 1950s hits included *Bye Bye Love, All I Have To Do Is Dream* and *Wake Up, Little Susie,* had joined the Marines Reserves in November last year to serve an initial six months' active service. Tonight, however, they were determined to 'plug' their new single, *Cryin' In The Rain* before reporting back for duty.

Five days later, older brother Don would marry Vanetia Stevenson, the former wife of film actor Russ Tamblyn - and *Cryin' In The Rain* would give The Everly Brothers yet another international Top 10 hit.

OAS Kill 12 In Algiers

The Secret Army of the OAS, composed of rebel French soldiers and French-Algerian settlers, increased their bid to delay independence for the North African state by killing 12 people today in the capital city of Algiers when it launched a major new bombing campaign.

Led by rebellious ex-General Raoul Salan, the OAS reacted violently when it was announced earlier in the month that peace talks were proceeding smoothly. Dozens of Muslims were assassinated in an attempt to provoke Arabs into a major confrontation which the OAS hoped would, in turn, result in French forces being called in to protect Europeans.

President de Gaulle's televized speech earlier in the month, in which he promised to bring peace to Algeria, was again looking difficult to fulfil, especially if the French Army - whose support would be vital - refused to co-operate.

MAR

French Army Capture OAS Leader In Algeria

French Army commanders following President de Gaulle's orders to crush the armed insurrection in Algeria were tonight celebrating the capture of a leading OAS military strategist, the French ex-General Edmond Jouhaud, along with a dozen of his retinue. They were arrested after a seven-hour battle in Oran.

After the signing of a peace treaty at Evian between France and the head of the provisional Algerian Government, Benyoussef Ben Kheddah, both Oran and the capital city, Algiers, had become little more than battlefields. Opposition to the treaty, which promised a referendum on the question of whether Algeria should become independent or remain tied to France, was typified by the orders given to OAS hard-liners by another rebel leader, former General Salan. He called for them to wage 'total war' on France and invited French soldiers to join his Secret Army.

Princess Grace In Screen Return?

There was intense excitement in film circles today when Princess Grace of Monaco confirmed that she was considering a return to the screen after six years away from Hollywood - as star of a new Alfred Hitchcock thriller, to be titled *Marnie*. As Grace Kelly, she was a star of the big screen in the first half of the 1950s, appearing in such memorable films as *High Noon, Dial M For Murder, Rear Window* and *The Country Girl,* for which she won an Oscar in 1954.

After enjoying huge success in *To Catch A Thief* with Cary Grant in 1955, and *High Society* with Bing Crosby and Frank Sinatra in 1956, she abandoned her cinematic career to marry Prince Rainier of Monaco.

Having previously rejected approaches to relaunch her film career, today's announcement was unexpected. It would also prove a false alarm. When shooting began on *Marnie,* in 1963, it would be without Princess Grace. The lead would be played by former TV model Tippi Hedren, who'd previously starred in Hitchcock's *The Birds.*

Liberal Party Win Reflects Government Unpopularity

IN ONE OF THE MOST UNEXPECTED political upsets in Britain for many years, the by-election in the quiet South London suburb of Orpington in Kent brought an unexpected and overwhelming victory for the Liberal Party candidate, Eric Lubbock.

At the last General Election, in 1959, the Conservative Party had won Orpington with a substantial majority of nearly 15,000 votes, but this was wiped out by Lubbock's new majority of almost 8000 - an unbelievable swing.

A spokesman for the vanquished tories called the result 'a flash in the pan', but it followed several other recent liberal successes, and some commentators speculated that Lubbock's victory could be the start of a return to a situation where British voters again had a choice between more than merely Labour or Tory candidates.

UK TOP 10 SINGLES

1: March Of The Siamese Children
- Kenny Ball's Jazzmen
2: Tell Me What He Said
- Helen Shapiro
3: Let's Twist Again
- Chubby Checker
4: Wonderful Land
- The Shadows
5: Can't Help Falling In Love
- Elvis Presley
6: Wimoweh
- Karl Denver
7: The Young Ones
- Cliff Richard
8: Rock-A-Hula-Baby
- Elvis Presley
9: Stranger On The Shore
- Acker Bilk
10: Hole In The Ground
- Bernard Cribbins

Fans Unsure About Shads With Strings

Although top British group The Shadows were in the process of enjoying an unprecedented eight weeks at the top of the British charts with *Wonderful Land,* written by Jerry Lordan, who also composed their first hit, *Apache,* in 1960, some of their fans weren't that happy with the new release.

The first Shadows single to feature orchestral backing, *Wonderful Land* was considered a bit slick, and maybe too much of a sell-out by those who preferred the group plain and simple - just two guitars, bass and drums. The rest of Britain didn't care and just bought it in its hundreds of thousands.

ARRIVALS

Born this month:

2: Jon Bon Jovi (Jon Biongiovi), US rock singer, songwriter, actor (Bon Jovi)

11: Lenny Wolf, British/US rock musician (Kingdom Come)

15: Terence Trent D'Arby, US pop/soul singer, songwriter

17: Claire Grogan, British pop musician, singer (Altered Images)

26: Richard Coles, British pop musician, music critic (The Communards, etc)

30: MC Hammer (Stanley Kirk Burrell), US rap/soul star

DEPARTURES

Died this month:

10: Sir Philip Armand Hamilton Gibbs, British author

23: Clement Davies, British politician

24: Auguste Piccard, Swiss deep-sea explorer and balloonist

Dylan Début Targets Folk Fans

The first album by the new US folk music sensation, Bob Dylan, was released this month to much excitement among his contemporaries in New York's Greenwich Village, as well as leading music journalists.

Simply titled *Bob Dylan,* it comprised of songs by black blues performers like Jesse Fuller, traditional folk songs which Dylan arranged to suit his style, plus a handful he wrote himself, including *Song To Woody* - a tribute to one of his heroes, the left-wing folk singer-activist Woody Guthrie.

Dylan's album was produced by Columbia Records' talent scout John Hammond, previously responsible for the 'discovery' of famous black jazz/blues vocalists Billie Holiday and Bessie Smith.

Goldwater targets US Far Right

A POLITICAL RALLY at Madison Square Garden in New York this evening confirmed the rise to prominence of - and growing substantial support for - revived right wing political policies, when Republican Senator Barry Goldwater was loudly applauded by a rally crowd of 20,000.

Goldwater, who had served as Senator for Arizona since 1953, was addressing an organization known as 'Young Americans For Freedom', though many were clearly not in the first flush of youth and all appeared determined to restrict the liberty of all who followed what they believed were the dangerously liberal philosophies of President Kennedy.

In fact, Goldwater - who was making an early attempt to raise his national profile before running for the US Presidency in 1964 - was naturally critical not only of President Kennedy in particular, but also of communism in general. Cheered on by his audience, the 53-year-old proclaimed that conservatism was, 'the wave of the future', calling it, 'young, virulent and alive'.

Jed And Co Quit Ozarks For Top Of US TV Charts

The critics jes' plumb hated it. 'Hopeless TV trash,' said one. 'Too absurd to be even slightly amusing,' said another, adding, 'At no time does it give the viewer credit for even a smattering of intelligence.'

Maybe it didn't, but *The Beverly Hillbillies* hit US television screens for the first time this month and became an instant No 1 ratings hit - a position it would hold for another two years. The show made household names out of Buddy Ebsen, Max Baer Jr, Irene Ryan and Donna Douglas - Jed Clampett, Jethro Bodine, Granny Daisy Moses and Elly May Clampett to you, cuzzin'.

Created by Paul Henning, *The Beverly Hillbillies* was destined to become a TV classic, with episodes recounting the misadventures of the suddenly-rich hicks providing television programmers around the world with a cult hit to this day.

ONLY 'LAWRENCE' SCORES AS BIG BUDGET MOVIES FLOP IN OSCARS

This year's Academy Awards bash in Hollywood proved an important point to the millions watching the glitterati from the safety of their TV lounges - the major studios may have still been able to force face-saving Best Picture nominations for films on which they'd lavished (and lost) the equivalant of many a Third World country's national debt, but they couldn't wangle a win for them.

Three of the year's most expensive films - *The Longest Day, The Music Man* and *Mutiny On The Bounty* - managed the rare achievement of being nominated as Best Picture without getting a single nomination in the categories logically essential to the creation of a picture so described: writing, directing and acting. The politics were so transparent, they were laughable.

Sam Spiegel was laughing, too. As producer of the one big budget blockbuster which did prove worthy of its Best Picture nomination by winning, *Lawrence of Arabia* was only the latest of a string of similar awards he'd won over the past 10 years - for *The African Queen, On The Waterfront, The Bridge On The River Kwai* and *Suddenly, Last Summer.* He'd collaborated with British director David Lean on *River Kwai,* so Lean's Best Director prize for Lawrence made their relationship doubly blessed.

For once, the acting Oscars went to performers who really did turn in superlative examples of their art. And, to drive the point home, only Gregory Peck's justified Best Actor award was given to a person in a nominated film - in his case, *To Kill A Mockingbird,* the excellent dramatization of Lee Harper's tense tale of Deep South small-town prejudice.

Competition for that was stiff, with Burt Lancaster (for *The Bird Man Of Alcatraz*), Jack Lemmon (*Days Of Wine And Roses*), Peter O'Toole (*Lawrence of Arabia*) and Marcello Mastroianni (*Divorce -Italian Style*) all in with a decent shout.

Anne Bancroft and Patty Duke's wondrous performances as teacher and multi-handicapped pupil in *The Miracle Worker* were recognized with Best Actress and

**Lawrence Olivier
in 'Lawrence of Arabia'**

Supporting Actress awards.

Bancroft's main rivals included the redoubtable Bette Davis (for *Whatever Happened To Baby Jane?*), Geraldine Page (*Sweet Bird Of Youth*) and Lee Remick (*Days Of Wine And Roses*), while the 16 year old Duke was pitched against relative veterans Angela Lansbury (*The Manchurian Candidate*), Thelma Ritter (*Bird Man Of Alcatraz*) and Mary Badham (*To Kill A Mockingbird*) in her category.

There was a puzzle in the Supporting Actor list won by Ed Begley for *Sweet Bird Of Youth*. Also nominated, for Billy Budd, was up-and-coming British actor Terence Stamp. As he played the title role, and featured in pretty well every scene, why on earth was he in competition as a supporting player?

There was no mystery attached to the Best Song award. Won last year by Henry Mancini and Johnny Mercer for their lovely *Moon River*, from the Audrey Hepburn movie *Breakfast At Tiffany's*, the two stepped up again this year to collect the same prize for *Days Of Wine And Roses* .

APRIL

Stirling Dices With Death At 110 mph

BRITISH MOTOR RACING ACE
Stirling Moss was rushed to the neurosurgical unit of a London hospital today after his *Lotus Climax* was involved in a 110 mph crash during a Formula One race at the Goodwood circuit in Sussex.

The 32-year-old, who had been second in the World Drivers Championship on four occasions, was again in second place in the 42-lap race - behind another British ace, Graham Hill - when he crashed. Knocked unconscious, Moss broke a rib and a leg besides incurring the serious head injuries which led to a high-speed ambulance dash into London.

The impact of the crash was so bad, it took rescue workers 30 minutes to free Moss from the wreckage. It was the end of what had already been a thrilling race for him as he nursed his ailing car past everyone except Hill, who eventually won the race. Thankfully, Stirling Moss would recover from his injuries.

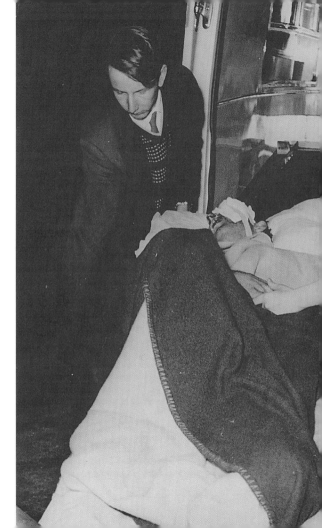

Satirist Cook Saves Threatened Eye

The outrageous but influential new British satirical magazine, *Private Eye,* whose continuing existence was in doubt after its turbulent first two months of life, was saved from extinction today, thanks to the action of fellow satirist Peter Cook. An instant favourite with London's students and style leaders, the magazine poked fun at establishment targets with scant regard for Britain's stringent libel laws, or any semblance of good taste. Just when it seemed as if the magazine, the brain child of former public schoolboy and founding editor Richard Ingram, was about to go under, Peter Cook - who'd enjoyed great success in London's West End and New York with the theatrical revue, *Beyond The Fringe,* with Alan Bennett, Jonathan Miller and Dudley Moore - stepped in as an investor. He would remain closely involved with *Private Eye,* through lawsuits and other near-disasters, until his death in 1995.

London Cops Get Flippers

London's Metropolitan Police force gained a new weapon in its unending fight against crime today, with the introduction of a frogman unit. Given how much of London's traffic and trade is carried by the River Thames as it runs through the heart of Britain's capital, it's only surprising that the new unit did not exist earlier to discover what - or who - was under its waters.

Commies To Be Barred From Whitehall?

The threat of political extremists infiltrating the Civil Service - the very heart of the British establishment - was tackled head-on today in London when the Radcliffe Report on security was published.

One of the most controversial proposals in the report, prepared by a government committee headed by Lord Radcliffe, recommended that members of the Communist Party should not be allowed to work in the Civil Service.

While an expected number of left-wing commentators naturally saw this as undemocratic, cynics asked just how many members of the Communist Party wishing to infiltrate the system would declare their membership, or their conversion, on job application forms?

UK TOP 10 SINGLES

1: Wonderful Land
- The Shadows

2: Hey! Baby
- Bruce Channel

3: Dream Baby
- Roy Orbison

4: When My Little Girl Is Smiling
- Jimmy Justice

5: Twistin' The Night Away
- Sam Cooke

6: Tell Me What He Said
- Helen Shapiro

7: Hey Little Girl
Del Shannon

8: Can't Help Falling In Love
- Elvis Presley

9: Never Goodbye
- Karl Denver

10: Speak To Me Pretty
- Brenda Lee

ARRIVALS
Born this month:
2: Billy Dean, US country singer, songwriter
6: Stan Cullimore, British pop musician (The Housemartins)
15: Nick Kamen, British model, actor
18: Shirlie Holliman, British pop singer (Pepsi & Shirlie)

DEPARTURES
Died this month:
5: Sir Percy Sillitoe, British intelligence chief, former head of MI6
10: Michael Curtiz (Mihaly Kertesz), Hungarian-born, Academy Award winning US film director (*Doctor X, Captain Blood, Yankee Doodle Dandy, Casablanca, Mildred Pierce, White Christmas, Young At Heart, King Creole*, etc)

Disguised Salan Snared In Algiers   APRIL 21

REPORTEDLY DISGUISED with an unconvincing false moustache and dyed hair, the leader of the OAS Secret Army in Algeria, disgraced ex-General Raoul Salan, was captured by French troops in Algiers today after being betrayed by one of his own followers.

Cornered in the bathroom of an apartment in central Algiers with his wife, her daughter and a trusted aide, former Captain Ferrandi, Salan at first denied his identity, but was still recognizable to the men who arrested him.

Salan was immediately rushed to a nearby military airbase and flown to Paris, where a cell in the Santé Prison was ready for him. Within hours, a street battle was being waged outside the prison between pro- and anti-OAS demonstrators after news of his capture was broadcast by French radio and TV stations.

Salan now faced trial on a variety of serious charges, not least that of treason, murder and military rebellion, all of which carried the death penalty.

Thirty Years For Bay Of Pigs Prisoners

Following the disastrous confrontation between the US and Cuba at the Bay Of Pigs in 1961, nearly 1200 members of the US and CIA-backed invasion force captured in the failed attempt to oust socialist President Fidel Castro were each sentenced to 30 years in prison by a court in the Cuban capital, Havana, today (see picture).

Castro, who swept to power in January 1959 when his guerrillas overwhelmed the forces of the Mafia and CIA-supported President Fulgencio Batistá, had an offer to make the US. He announced that he would accept a ransom payment of $62 million for the release of the men sentenced today.

Budget Cuts Prices To Tempt British Consumers

The British Chancellor of The Exchequer, Selwyn Lloyd, slashed purchase tax on household goods and cars today when he delivered his Budget for the new financial year - moves which economists predicted would lead to a much-needed boom in the British economy.

The Chancellor's 10 per cent cut in purchase tax reduced the cost of a Mini car to under £500 ($1500), for instance, and made a new Rolls-Royce £600 ($1800) cheaper. An even greater boom was expected in sales of television sets, washing-machines and refrigerators.

Critics of the Budget expressed fears of an increase in the use of hire purchase and in imported goods. Mr Lloyd dismissed those fears and had a trick up his sleeve to ensure British children didn't share their parents' joy at price cuts. He introduced a new 15 per cent tax on confectionery and ice-cream.

France And Belgium Back British EEC Bid

Britain's bid to join the European Economic Community - the Common Market - received a boost from an unexpected source today when French and Belgian ministers meeting in Paris called for Britain's application to be accepted.

The EEC was formed in Rome in 1957, when France, West Germany, Italy, Belgium, Holland and Luxembourg united to create a union allowing the free movement of people, goods and money between member states, and abolishing all trade tariffs.

Britain chose not to join the club, preferring instead to form a European Free Trade Association with Austria, Denmark, Norway, Portugal, Sweden and Switzerland in 1959. British Prime Minister Harold Macmillan always believed that Britain should have been an EEC member from the start, though he knew he faced opposition from President de Gaulle.

Tears In Court As Salan's Life Is Spared

THE TRIAL of ex-General Raoul Salan, the admitted leader of the OAS Secret Army which had brought murder and mayhem to both Algeria and mainland France, ended in chaos and tears of relief today when, despite a guilty verdict, the traitorous rebel was not sentenced to death.

To the amazement of prosecuting lawyers, journalists, most of the French population - and the defendant himself - the president of the military tribunal said that due to unexplained, mitigating circumstances, Salan was only being sentenced to life imprisonment.

The verdict moved Salan to tears, especially understandable as another OAS conspirator, ex-General Jouhaud, had been moved to death row only days earlier. As the truth hit him, his tears turned to hysterical laughter.

Salan's unexpected reprieve was a special victory for Maitre Tixier-Vignancour, a right-wing lawyer who'd successfully pleaded for clemency for the wartime collaborator, Marshal Pétain when he faced trial in 1946. He persuaded the court that sentencing Salan to death

would promote considerable uproar in France.

During the course of the trial, Secret Army supporters had publicly threatened to kill the judges if their erstwhile leader was sent to the guillotine. In addition, a band of asassins from Algeria, whose mission was to kill President de Gaulle, were apprehended by security forces.

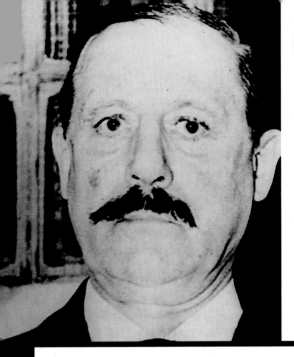

Panic As NASA Mislays Astronaut

Confusion reigned at NASA flight control in Houston, Texas, today when US astronaut Lieutenant Commander Scott Carpenter and his *Aurora 5* space capsule went out of contact with mission controllers for almost an hour after re-entry into the earth's atmosphere.

The second US orbital space voyage missed the area in which it was supposed to land by over 200 miles, but both Carpenter and his capsule were finally discovered and retrieved after the pilot had spent three hours on a life raft in the sea.

The test flight brought several potential problems to light which enabled scientists to make corrections for future expeditions away from the earth. Carpenter apparently made two small, but crucial mistakes during the re-entry process, and also depleted the spaceship's hydrogen supply by using too much power in certain manoeuvres.

UK TOP 10 SINGLES

1: Wonderful Land
- The Shadows
2: Hey! Baby
- Bruce Channel
3: Dream Baby
- Roy Orbison
4: When My Little Girl Is Smiling
- Jimmy Justice
5: Twistin' The Night Away
- Sam Cooke
6: Tell Me What He Said
- Helen Shapiro
7: Hey Little Girl
- Del Shannon
8: Can't Help Falling In Love
- Elvis Presley
9: Never Goodbye
- Karl Denver
10: Speak To Me Pretty
- Brenda Lee

German Pensioners Tunnel To Freedom

The Berlin Wall proved no obstacle to a band of eleven senior citizens from East Berlin, who today excavated a tunnel underneath the barrier separating the communist-governed Eastern sector from the West and used it to escape.

The underground walkway, which took them two weeks to dig, was six feet (about two metres) from floor to ceiling.

Why was it so high? As the 81-year-old leader of the group, which included four women, explained to curious reporters, 'We did not want our wives to crawl, but to walk unbowed to freedom.'

MAY 25

Coventry's New Cathedral Rises From The Ashes

A six-year project which cost nearly £1.5 million ($5 million) came to a glorious climax today with the consecration of the new Coventry Cathedral (pictured), built alongside the ancient church which was destroyed by bombs at the height of World War II.

Designed by Sir Basil Spence, who won the design contract in competition with other leading international architects, the new building was connected to the ruins of the old cathedral by a pillared porch.

Two of the major features incorporated into the new cathedral were huge pieces of sacred art, each of which was more than 60 feet (18 metres) high. A massive tapestry by Graham Sutherland depicted Christ surrounded by the four beasts described in the book of Revelation, while a huge stained-glass window was the inspired creation of artist John Piper.

The bold and modern style of the building and its ornamentation was not, of course, to everyone's tastes. Typically, a large sculpture of St Michael vanquishing the devil which dominated the cathedral's main entrance - the work of Jacob Epstein - came in for more than its fair share of criticism from traditionalists.

MAY 30

Nikita Bops To Benny

Russian leader Nikita Khrushchev was one of 3000 Muskovites who packed a concert hall tonight to see and hear the legendary jazz clarinettist Benny Goodman in his Russian début.
Introduced to the US musician after the show, which won a standing ovation from jazz-loving comrades lucky enough to buy, beg or bribe themselves tickets, Mr Khrushchev admitted that while he'd been 'pleased' with Goodman's concert, some of the music played had left him a little puzzled.

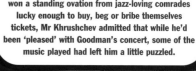

Kennedy Sends US Marines To South-East Asia

President John Kennedy today ordered infantry and marines from the US Seventh Fleet into Siam (later known as Thailand) in response to the growing communist threat in South-East Asia from Pathet Lao forces in the neighbouring country of Laos.

The US was expected to request members of the South-East Asia Treaty Organization (SEATO) to provide additional support for its 5000 military personnel, although such SEATO additions would be deployed more for political reasons than to bolster US strength. While there was little doubt that US strength would be sufficient to quell Pathet Lao forces, the presence of SEATO allies was needed to convince the Siamese people of international support in case of need.

One of President Kennedy's main stated aims was to avert communist-backed revolutions in South-East Asia, particularly in Vietnam and Siam.

Holocaust Architect Eichmann Pays Ultimate Penalty

CONVICTED NAZI WAR CRIMINAL Adolf Eichmann, the Gestapo officer who admitted to having been the organizational brains behind the wartime slaughter of millions of Jews in Hitler's concentration camps, was finally executed just before midnight tonight in Israel.

Eichmann's appeal for clemency was rejected, and his last request was for a bottle of wine. He wrote letters to members of his family, and was visited by a British clergyman before being escorted to the scaffold from which he was hung.

Rejecting the traditional black hood, he told witnesses, 'We shall meet again. I have believed in God. I obeyed the rules of war and was loyal to my flag,' and named Germany, Argentina (where he had been in hiding before being captured by Israeli intelligence men) and Austria as countries he would not forget.

Eichmann - a former travelling salesman for a vacuum-cleaner company, a one-time guard at Dachau, and a Lieutenant-Colonel in the SS when the war ended - was not a man the people of Israel would ever forget, either.

JUNE 25

Film Star Sophia Wed To Bigamist?

INTERNATIONALLY ADMIRED Italian film queen Sophia
Loren was again the subject of front-page headlines today when she
learned that she and her husband, the film producer Carlo Ponti,
were to face charges that their five-year marriage was bigamous.

According to a Rome magistrate, their marriage by proxy in
Mexico was illegal. Although Ponti had obtained a divorce there
from his first wife, Italian law did not allow or recognize divorce.
Ergo, he was still married, was a bigamist by definition, and La Loren
- as an Italian citizen bound by the same laws - was a bigamist too!

While the disruption meant the Academy Award winning star was
forced to cancel plans to film in London later in the year, she chose
to complete her current film project in Italy. 'I have never run away
from anything,' she told journalists.

In fact, the couple would eventually leave Italy and set up home in
the relative calm of Switzerland, their marriage surviving intact in
international law.

JUNE 8

OAS Ignites Algerian Oil Fields

French OAS rebels hit the economy of Algeria - the country they were fighting to
keep part of France - hard today when they torched desert oil fields in a desperate
attempt to regain the initiative after the conviction of their leaders.

Using plastic explosives, the terrorists ignited oil wells in the Sahara, almost the
sole source of Algerian international trade.

This outrage followed a conflagration at the University of Algiers and the deaths of
four Muslims who were gunned down in the capital.

JUNE 4

Liverpool Quartet Sign With EMI

The most popular pop group in their Liverpool home town, but unknown in London, The Beatles signed a provisional contract with EMI Records today to begin making test recordings with producer George Martin.

The quartet - John Lennon, Paul McCartney, George Harrison and new drummer Ringo Starr - had been rejected by Decca Records after an audition in January, but were optimistic that the material they recorded with Martin would persuade EMI executives to take them on full-time.

JUNE 17

Brazil (Without Pelé) Win World Cup

Brazil emerged as World Cup Champions again today in the Chilean capital, Santiago, when they beat Czechoslovakia 3-1. And they did it without their superstar striker Pelé who was out of action with a pulled muscle.

The tournament was marred by violence and sendings-off, but served to confirm the complete superiority of the Brazilian squad. *(See Sports pages for full details)*

JUNE 11

Moguls Cancel Monroe Film

The always-controversial life of actress Marilyn Monroe took another bleak turn today when studio bosses at 20th Century Fox cancelled production on the film she and Dean Martin had just started. They were, it was said, unhappy with early 'rushes' and Monroe's apparent inability to keep up with the production schedule. Production of *Something's Got To Give,* which was being directed by George Cukor, would be abandoned when Dean Martin refused to work with a different co-star. This caused other workers on the film, who were incensed by the decision, to pay for an advertisement in Variety magazine 'thanking' Marilyn for losing them their jobs.

Vita, Green-Fingered Writer, Dies

VICTORIA SACKVILLE-WEST, the noted essayist and horticulturalist who had recently celebrated her 70th birthday, died today at Sissinghurst Castle, the former ruin she and her diplomat husband, Sir Harold Nicholson had rebuilt, and whose gardens became her life's work and greatest triumph.

Vita, as she was universally known, was a close friend of the controversial author Virginia Woolf, who was said to have based the sex-change heroine/hero of her novel *Orlando* on her bisexual chum.

Vita's other major legacy to the world was her skill as a gardener, and the results of her green-fingered genius can still be admired at Sissinghurst Castle near Sevenoaks in Kent.

JUNE 26

Moffit Takes Wimbledon Crown

A new star emerged at this year's Wimbledon Tennis Championships when the top seed, Australian Margaret Smith, was beaten by an 18-year-old US newcomer in the Ladies Singles.

Miss Smith's position as favourite for the title was overturned when she was beaten by the bespectacled teenager, Billie-Jean Moffit. However, Miss Moffit did not win the Ladies crown for 1962. That went to another American, Karen Susman, who beat Czech champion Valentina Sukova 6-4, 6-4.

JUNE 30

Gentlemen Transformed Into Players

A particularly English social/sporting tradition came to an overdue end today with the announcement that the annual cricket match between Gentlemen and Players would be the last in a series which began in 1806.

The distinction between professional cricketers (who earned a living from the sport) and amateurs (who theoretically participated for the pleasure of playing the game, rather than for financial reward) was abolished with the end of the Gentlemen versus Players games.

Many in the game felt that the writing had appeared on the wall when Yorkshireman Len Hutton became the first professional (or Player) to be appointed as captain of the England team back in 1953.

NO PELE, BUT BRAZIL BEAT DARK-HORSE CZECHS

The presence of the largely unfancied Czechoslovakia in this year's World Cup final in Chile was an obvious surprise to all the pundits who'd predicted the host nation, West Germany or Argentina to make it to the big showdown with reigning champions Brazil.

As it was, the Czechs (who'd been drawn in the same group as Brazil), had fully earned their place of honour by beating Spain 1-0, drawing 0-0 with Brazil and stumbling to a 1-3 defeat by Mexico to go through to the quarter-finals where they'd beaten Hungary 1-0 to win a semi-final match against a surging Yugoslavia, who'd they'd comprehensively humbled 3-1.

Brazil, for their part, had been without their maestro, Pele, since he was injured in their first group game against Mexico, a blow not even their 2-0 win on that day could soften. Their goal-less draw with Czechoslovakia and a 2-1 win over Spain had given them a game with England in the quarter-finals, which they duly won 2-1 to end the best England World Cup run since 1954.

Confronted with their Chilean hosts - and a vast and naturally partisan crowd - in the semi-final, Brazil had stormed to a 4-2 victory against a team which had been involved in a disgraceful group tie with Italy marked by two-footed tackles, spitting and fighting. It was remarkable that British referee Ken Aston sent only two players off in a game which all agreed marked a new low for world-class soccer.

The final, in contrast, was a superb game which the Czechs enlivened hugely with an opening 16th minute goal from Masopust. Shaken by this affront, Brazil went on the offensive, and it was only a matter of minutes before Pele's replacement, Amarildo, had equalled the score.

It was not until the 69th minute that Brazil's 30 year-old midfield genius Zito put them ahead. Brazil made sure of retaining their title when the Czeck 'keeper, Schroiff, fumbled a speculative (or brilliant) lob sent in by centre-forward Vava. The only real surprise was the absence from the scoresheet of Brazil's Garrincha who - along with team-mate Vava, Chile's Sanchez, Yugoslavia's Jerkovic, Hungary's Albert and the Soviet Union's Ivanov - was the tournament's leading goal scorer, with an eventual tally of four.

MOSS - STIRLING BY NAME AND NATURE

The horrific Goodwood crash which almost cost Stirling Moss his life this Easter also ended a brilliant career which was all the more remarkable because Moss was arguably the best driver never to win the world championship.

He came darned close a few times - in 1955, '56 and '57 he was second to the immortal Juan Fangio (so no disgrace there), while a last-race breakdown cost him the point by which Mike Hawthorn pipped him in 1958. On another two occasions he finished third. He also amassed a creditable 16 wins in his 66 Grand Prix races between 1951-56 to end his Formula One career with 186.64 points.

Admired and respected by foes and fans alike, Stirling Moss was the first Englishman to win the British Grand Prix (in 1955, the year he joined Fangio in the Mercedes team) and, while racing a sports car in the same year, was the first to win the gruelling Italian Mille Miglia.

Awarded the OBE in 1959, Moss was - above all - a hugely enthusiastic man who would not let a small thing like an official retirement stop him, in later years, climbing behind the wheel of something very fast to raise money for charity.

It's a measure of the impact he made on the British consciousness that, for fully a decade after he'd been forced to retire, the most common question asked of drivers by traffic cops who'd ordered them to the road-side was: 'Who do you think you are - Stirling Moss?'

PACKERS DENY TITTLE'S GIANTS - AGAIN

In 1961, YA Tittle had led the New York Giants to the NFL Championship game against a young Green Bay Packers team who'd comprehensively stomped him and his best players into a humiliating 37-0 shut-down.

This season's championship tussle once again pitched Tittle (always known merely by his initials, which stood for an understandably-abbreviated Yelberton Abraham!) and the Giants against the Packers. This year, however, the Giants' quarterback had reason to be more confident.

During the season he'd thrown 33 scoring strikes to lead the league. His arm was in, his runners were on-form, so what could the Vince Lombardi-coached Packers do against that?

The answer, to be brief, was: beat the Giants again! Although the Giants would at least get on the board with seven points, Vince Lombardi's crew put together sixteen to take the trophy which would - in later years - be named after him.

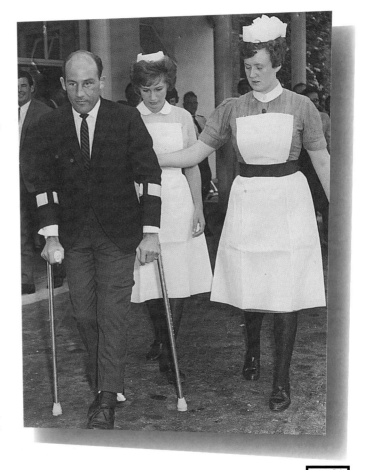

JULY

Fascist Mosley Returns To Riots

SIR OSWALD MOSLEY, the 62-year-old British politician who left the socialist Labour Party to found the pro-Nazi British Union of Fascists in 1932, once again encountered violent opposition to his views today in London's East End when he was attacked by demonstrators who knocked him to the ground and punched him.

Mosley was attempting to address a meeting of the neo-fascist Union Movement, which was brought to a premature end by police after less than five minutes, as a barrage of objects and abuse were hurled at him. Over fifty people were arrested for breaches of the peace.

This was the second such anti-Mosley demonstration within a week and followed a violent confrontation between Mosleyite 'Blackshirts' and demonstrators at a rally in London's

Trafalgar Square. Mosley laid the blame at government failure to control what he called 'Red anarchy'.

There was also a noticeable rise in extreme right-wing activity in other parts of Britain, with the formation

of the British Nazi Party (BNP), whose anti-semitic philosophy echoed events in World War II. A mob of several hundred white racists was reported to have launched a march on black immigrants living in Dudley, Worcestershire.

1: I Can't Stop Loving You
- Ray Charles

2: A Picture Of You
- Joe Brown & The Bruvvers

3: Come Outside
- Mike Sarne and Wendy Richard

4: I Remember You
- Frank Ifield

5: Good Luck Charm
- Elvis Presley

6: Here Comes That Feeling
- Brenda Lee

7: English Country Garden
- Jimmie Rodgers

8: Ginny Come Lately
- Brian Hyland

9: Don't Ever Change
- The Crickets

10: Speedy Gonzales
- Pat Boone

JULY 26

Kennedy Cool Towards Laotian Leader

The Washington administration's reaction to the official visit begun today by the leader of Laos's new left-right coalition government, Prince Souvanna Phouma, could only be described as cool, despite the fact that the coalition had resulted in improved, if only temporary, political stability.

The prince was in Washington to discuss the provision of US aid for Laos after international pressure had forced the country's two opposing factions into a power-sharing settlement.

President Kennedy's reluctance to extend a warm welcome to him was based on the prince's clear allegiance to the Pathet Lao communists with whom the US forces were still locked in jungle warfare.

JULY 3

De Gaulle Grants Independence To Algeria

After a referendum which gave overwhelming support to the motion that Algeria should become an independent state with help from France, President Charles de Gaulle today confirmed that Algeria should no longer be treated as a French colony.

The referendum - in which six million votes were cast, with 99 per cent saying 'Oui' - involved both French and Arab citizens, and ended a long and bloody conflict which had forced de Gaulle to come out of retirement to take charge again.

Hovercraft Links England And Wales

JULY 20

A new age in passenger transport was born today when a hovercraft service opened between the North Wales resort of Rhyl and the Lancashire town of Wallasey.

Twenty-four paying passengers made the first trip across the estuary of the River Dee, along with two postal-sacks containing some 8000 letters and greeting cards from Rhyl Chamber of Commerce members to the great and good of Wallasey.

ARRIVALS

Born this month:
7: Clive Jackson, British pop musician (Dr & The Medics)
20: Dig Wayne, British rock musician (Jo Boxers)
28: Rachel Sweet, US rock singer, songwriter

DEPARTURES

Died this month:
4: John Christie, British founder of Glyndebourne Opera
6: William Harrison Faulkner, US novelist
21: George Macaulay Trevelyan, British historian
27: Richard Aldington, British novelist, biographer

JULY 10

Martin Luther King Jailed

The continuing struggle to win racial integration in the US's Deep South claimed the liberty of civil rights leader Dr Martin Luther King once more today when he was arrested during a protest in Georgia.

At City Hall in Albany, Georgia, Dr King was trying to persuade the town's mayor to hold negotiations which had been promised eight months before, but repeatedly postponed. Both he and the Rev Ralph Abernathy, a fellow cleric who had been arrested for similar offences twice in the previous six months, were taken to jail when they tried to hold a prayer meeting after being told that the mayor was away.

They, and more than 20 other civil rights workers, were then charged with causing a disturbance.

Macmillan Decimates Cabinet In Night Of Long Knives

BRITISH PRIME MINISTER Harold Macmillan dismissed seven members of his cabinet tonight after the Conservative Party's latest disastrous defeat in a Parliamentary by-election. Among those summarily sacked during what soon became known as The Night of the Long Knives, was Chancellor of the Exchequer Selwyn Lloyd.

Political commentators could not recall a more brutal piece of pruning than Macmillan's, and generally agreed that he appeared to have been panicked into the action by an electoral defeat which only confirmed the unpopularity of his government's pay restraints policy.

There was also known to be increasing disquiet in the ranks of the previously loyal Conservative Party - a mood Macmillan obviously hoped would change in the face of what he called 'a broad reconstruction'. Later in the month, he would announce the formation of a National Incomes Commission to vet wage claims.

Leading Liberal MP Jeremy Thorpe, whose party had benefited from the collapse of the tory vote, caused much amusement with a clever quote about the cabinet clean-out - 'Greater love hath no man than this, that he lay down his friends for his life.'

Laver Wins All-Oz Wimbledon

Rod Laver, the dynamic red-haired Australian darling of the world tennis circuit, retained his Wimbledon championship title today - and proved his complete superiority - by taking only 50 minutes to do it. Facing fellow Australian Marty Mulligan, the brilliant left-handed amateur ace powered his way to a resounding 6-2, 6-2, 6-1 victory as emphatic as any ever seen on the famous Centre Court.

US Watches Live TV From Europe Via Telstar

Television images were transmitted across the Atlantic for the first time today, through the new communications satellite, Telstar.

A picture of the chairman of AT&T, the company which constructed the satellite, was appropriately the first thing transmitted across the Atlantic, after which a live performance by French entertainer Yves Montand was transmitted into US homes.

It was early days for satellite broadcasting, with programme times limited by the fact that Telstar had to be actually passing over the country from which the pictures were sent before the system could work.

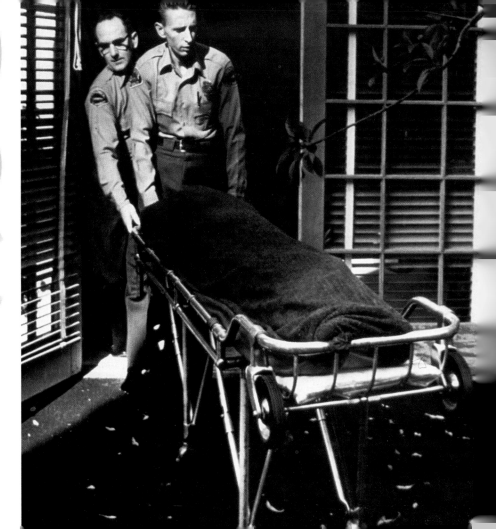

World Mourns Screen Goddess Marilyn

THE FILM WORLD lost one of its most potent icons tonight when the 36-year-old star and sex symbol Marilyn Monroe was discovered dead in the bed of her Hollywood bungalow by her housekeeper, Eunice Murray.

Mrs Murray called Miss Monroe's personal physician, Dr Ralph Greenson, after she saw lights on in the house at 3 am and was unable to get an answer to her telephone call. It was he who alerted emergency services. Dr Greenson had spoken to Marilyn a few hours earlier when she complained of insomnia - an empty bottle of sleeping tablets was found beside her bed.

Marilyn's problems with sleeplessness were confirmed by director John Huston, who had worked on *The Misfits* - which turned out to be the last of her 22 film appearances and the farewell of co-star Clark Gable. 'Only God knows why she was so afraid of not being able to sleep,' he said.

Only three months earlier, she had been sacked from the film *Something's Got To Give,* because she was regarded as unreliable by 20th Century Fox studios.

Brought up by foster parents, Norma Jean Baker (her real name) was married three times, first at the age of 16, next to the famous US baseball star, Joe Di Maggio, and finally to playwright Arthur Miller, but she was seemingly never able to find true happiness, despite the adoration of millions.

Reliant on a mixture of drugs to function properly, she was known to have had affairs with both President John Kennedy and his brother Bobby. Those facts would combine to fuel a conspiracy theory about Marilyn's death which continues to this day, while her fragile beauty still stares down from the thousands of posters which are sold worldwide.

King And Abernathy Freed Amid Protests

Only two weeks after city officials in Albany, Georgia, locked US civil rights leaders Dr Martin Luther King and the Rev Ralph Abernathy up for ignoring police orders to move off the steps of City Hall, they and 28 others were ordered to be released today.

Their freedom came as the city faced a massive protest march and widespread breaking of local segregation laws. It was the third time the two had been arrested by southern States' authorities since January.

UK TOP 10 SINGLES

1: I Remember You
- Frank Ifield
2: Speedy Gonzales
- Pat Boone
3: Guitar Tango
- The Shadows
4: Things
- Bobby Darin
5: I Can't Stop Loving You
- Ray Charles
6: Roses Are Red
- Ronnie Carroll
7: A Picture Of You
- Joe Brown & The Bruvvers
8: Don't Ever Change
- The Crickets
9: Once Upon A Dream
- Billy Fury
10: Little Miss Lonely
- Helen Shapiro

Britain Expels US Nazi Rockwell

In London to link with British neo-Nazis in a bid to create an international racist and anti-semitic network, George Rockwell - the leader of the US Nazi Party - found himself under arrest tonight and on his way to Heathrow Airport in the company of Special Branch officers.

Rockwell, whose arrival in Britain caused an uproar when civil liberties groups heard of his visit, was put on the next flight back to New York, and firmly advised that he should cancel any future plans he may have had of returning.

ARRIVALS

Born this month:

4: Paul Reynolds, British pop musician (A Flock Of Seagulls); Mark O'Connor, US country music multi-instrumentalist, arranger

5: Tracy Edwards, British international yachtswoman

15: Marshal Schofield, British pop musician (The Fall)

23: Shaun Ryder, British pop musician (Happy Mondays)

DEPARTURES

Died this month:

5: Marilyn Monroe, US film actress *(see main story)*

9: Herman Hesse, German novelist, poet *(Steppenwolf, Narziss and Goldmund,* etc)

AUGUST 13

British Climbers Conquer North Face Of Eiger

The treacherous north face of the Eiger Mountain was successfully scaled by British climbers today when Chris Bonnington and Ian Clough, both in their twenties, conquered the 13,000-feet Swiss peak in only two days, making their ascent one of the fastest ever completed.

  Although they achieved their goal with relative ease and their two days away from civilization were apparently trouble-free - they later said it had been a 'very enjoyable climb, with no difficulties' - others attempting the same feat were less fortunate. Two others, one a Scot, were killed, bringing the number of fatalities this year alone to more than two dozen.

Teenager Left To Die On Berlin Wall

ON THE FIRST ANNIVERSARY of the construction of the Berlin Wall which separated the east and western sectors of Germany's former capital, thousands of demonstrators from West Berlin marched in protest against the infamous barrier and the brutal killing - a day earlier - of an East German teenager.

Peter Frechter was trying to climb the Wall to escape from the Eastern sector, when he was shot in the back by East German guards with machine guns, and simply bled to death while his killers looked on.

West German police and horrified onlookers were unable to reach Frechter to provide assistance, other than by throwing bandages to him as he called vainly for help.

The spot where Peter Frechter died was later marked by a wooden cross and a pile of flowers. A sign attached to the cross simply said, 'We accuse'.

De Gaulle Cheats Assassins Again

Assassins from the outlawed French-Algerian OAS Secret Army today failed - for the fourth time in 12 months - to kill President Charles de Gaulle. Ironically, he was attacked as he left a cabinet meeting to discuss methods of curbing terrorism. The President was near Versailles in his official car, *en route* to an airport on the outskirts of Paris, when the terrorists struck. Machine-gun fire came from three directions, but the only damage sustained was to the car.

Despite its two punctured tyres and a shattered window, the car was swiftly driven to a rendezvous over a mile away where de Gaulle, his wife and their son-in-law transferred to another vehicle.

Russians Stick Together In Space

Russian space scientists celebrated today as they confirmed that, for the first time in the space race, simultaneous orbits of the earth were being undertaken by two Russian cosmonauts in different spacecraft.

One of the men involved, Major Andrian Nikolayev, already held the record for spending the longest time in space, having orbited the earth more than 30 times. His *Vostok* spacecraft had been launched two days before that of his compatriot, Lieutenant Colonel Pavel Popovitch.

It was hoped that there might be an opportunity for the two rockets to be connected together in orbit, which would have been another important achievement in the continuing exploration of space.

BARRIERS TUMBLE AS BLUESMAN CHARLES GOES COUNTRY

It's impossible to overstate just how important Ray Charles' decision to record an album of country and western material late in 1961 was to the world of popular music. It wasn't merely that a black performer was 'covering' the whitest of white southern music at a time when the American South was torn by racial conflict, but that it was Ray Charles, current king of the R&B and soul fields.

Like most musicians, Ray Charles didn't acknowledge any barriers when it came to music. If a song was strong and he could twist it to his own distinctive styling and phrasing, he never cared if the author was black, white or puce. Anyway, if young white southern kids like Elvis Presley, Carl Perkins and Jerry Lee Lewis could borrow freely from black music to make rock 'n' roll…

The fact was, as Charles would patiently explain to anyone who asked, he'd grown up in Georgia with the family radio tuned in to hillbilly stations as often as it had been to gospel or blues. It was his music too.

Born Ray Charles Robinson, in Albany, Georgia, and blinded by measles at the age of six, he'd learned to play piano as a pupil at St Augustine's School for the Deaf and Blind in Orlando, Florida, and - at the age of 17 - was leading his own jazz trio in Seattle.

Between 1952 and 1959, Charles had become one of the most popular and influential artists on the infant Atlantic Records label and the US concert and festival circuits. Hits like *It Should've Been Me, I Got A Woman, This Little Girl Of Mine, Hallelujah I Love Her So* and *What'd I Say* had made him a superstar. Interestingly, in 1959 he'd enjoyed a sizeable pop chart hit with *I'm Moving On,* his very distinctive version of a Hank Snow country and western hit.

Modern Sounds In Country And Western Music would not only top the US album charts for 14 weeks in 1962, selling more than a million copies in the process, but it would produce singles chart hits on both sides of the Atlantic with *Unchain My Heart* (a US Top 10 hit in January), *I Can't Stop Loving You* (a US No 1 for five weeks from June and America's biggest-selling single of 1962, and UK No 1 in July), *You Don't Know Me* (US Top 10 in August and September, and UK Top 10 in September), while he'd score US Top 20 hits with both *Your Cheating Heart* and *You Are My Sunshine* in December.

The roll would continue well into 1963 as a *Modern Sounds Vol 2* album delivered a huge international hit with *Take These Chains From My Heart*. Ray Charles would return to Nashville at various times in the future, but he'd made his point for the time being: Music has no colour.

IT'S TRAD, DAD AS KENNY AND ACKER SCORE

That 1962 should witness a revival of traditional jazz was weird enough, but that the revival would produce two of the year's biggest-selling singles around the world was doubly so. Add the fact that those records were made by white British musicians and their bands, and we're into serious *Outer Limits* territory.

The hits were, of course, *Midnight In Moscow* and *Stranger On The Shore,* and the artists responsible were, respectively, trumpeter Kenny Ball and clarinettist Acker Bilk. The fact that neither were traditional jazz tunes need not concern us. The fact is, both led bands which generally played it strictly trad yet packed Britain's biggest concert and dance halls every bit as easily as the biggest pop idols!

The Essex born Kenny Ball was 31 this year, had already been pro for ten years and leader of his own Kenny Ball's Jazzmen for four years. Released in the US in February, *Midnight In Moscow* fairly raced up the charts to arrive at No 1 in March and win Kenny Ball a gold disc for a million-plus sales.

In Britian *Midnight In Moscow* had been shadowed at every turn by Acker Bilk's *Stranger On The Shore,* a haunting clarinet and strings production which had become the UK No 1 in January this year. As the 33- year-old Somerset-born Acker (real name Bernard) saw his rival's hit climbing the US charts, he must have thought he was also in with a chance of topping his track record of eight previous UK hits by finally scoring in America.

It did - and how! Finally released in April, when Ball's record had started to drop, *Stranger On The Shore* would spend all of May and June as the US No 2 single - held off the top by Ray Charles' multi-million selling *I Can't Stop Loving You.*

The trad revival would be over as quickly as it had flared up, but not before a formula movie, *It's Trad, Dad!,* had been made to embarrass everyone concerned in later years. Ball and Bilk would return to long and successful club and cabaret careers, their five minutes of international fame brilliantly exploited.

ADAM'S FANS KEEP THE FAITH

One burning question as 1962 dawned was, could Adam Faith possibly continue the remarkable run of hits he'd enjoyed since his arrival on the UK pop scene in November 1959 with the No 1 hit *What Do You Want?* Since then he'd notched up a further chart-topper with *Poor Me,* six Top 10 hits and two which only just missed out, both making No 12.

Second only to Cliff Richard as far as teen worship was concerned, the 22-year-old Londoner with the Buddy

Adam Faith - a remarkable run of hits

Holly hiccup in his voice and the unusual French college boy haircut needed to come up with something special if he wasn't - like so many of those who'd come up behind Cliff - to fade from the charts.

The answer was unconditional as Faith ran up a new string of four big hits in 1962 to keep the pot boiling - *Lonesome, As You Like It, Don't That Beat All* and *What Now.*

Already having appeared in three feature films (*Never Let Go, Beat Girl* and *What A Whopper!*), he ended 1962 working on *Mix Me A Person* with Anne Baxter and Donald Sinden, signalling the direction his career would take when his teen-idol days were done.

SEPT

Liston Smash-And-Grabs World Heavyweight Crown

THE WORLD HAD A NEW and fearsome heavyweight boxing champion tonight when 30-year-old Sonny Liston took the title by knocking out defending champion Floyd Patterson in the first round of their fight in Chicago.

Using his fists like clubs, Liston landed several awesome blows which forced the title holder into the ropes, then to the canvas, where he was counted out after a little over two minutes of what was scheduled to be a 15-round fight.

Patterson had taken the crown from Swedish champion Ingemar Johansson in June 1960, when he became the first world heavyweight champion ever to regain the title. But Liston was no respecter of reputation, and he lived up to his own less-than-spotless reputation - which included innumerable brushes with the law as a wayward and violent teenager in Arkansas - by becoming the first man this century to take a world championship via a knockout in the first round.

Bomb Spoils Nkrumah's Celebration

The continuing threat to the life of Ghanaian President Kwame Nkrumah was emphasized tonight when assassins made another unsuccessful attempt to kill him. Ironically, the new threat came at a party attended by 2000 guests to celebrate the President's escape from a murder plot last month.

One person was killed and a number of others injured when a bomb exploded outside Flagstaff House, the presidential residence in Accra, capital of Ghana.

Nkrumah's two-year administration was regularly threatened by violent opponents, but tonight's bomb was blamed on a fresh group of militants, the Kumasi Command. Nkrumah's response was to arrest hundreds of political opponents all over Ghana.

Cuba Crisis - Kennedy Given Permission To Mobilize Military

In view of escalating concern about the political stand-off between the US and Cuba - geographically neighbours, but philosophically worlds apart - President Kennedy was being given fresh powers by Congress today.

In case of need, he would be able to call up troops from the national reserve without declaring a state of emergency, a previous prerequisite for such action. The President's enhanced authority came after Russian leader Nikita Khrushchev's threat that a US attack on Cuba would result in nuclear war.

The crisis, which had put the entire US military machine on a war-preparedness footing, followed US Secretary of State Dean Rusk's charge that Russian nuclear missiles had been sited in Cuba.

Southern Rhodesia's PM Bans Black Nationalists

The Zimbabwe African People's Union (ZAPU) - Southern Rhodesia's black nationalist organization - was outlawed today by the Prime Minister, Sir Edgar Whitehead, and branded as a terrorist organization.

ZAPU had been targeting black opponents of its aims to gain equal political rights for the country's majority black African population, and Southern Rhodesia's independence. Tribal chiefs in remote country areas had especially suffered, with petrol bombs and incendiary devices exploding in churches, schools and private residences. Armed police rounded up ZAPU bosses, while troops were deployed to guard power stations and airfields.

UK TOP 10 SINGLES

1: She's Not You
- Elvis Presley
2: I Remember You
- Frank Ifield
3: Roses Are Red
- Ronnie Carroll
4: It'll Be Me
- Cliff Richard
5: Things
- Bobby Darin
6: Sealed With A Kiss
- Brian Hyland
7: Breaking Up Is Hard To Do
- Neil Sedaka
8: Telstar
- The Tornados
9: Speedy Gonzales
- Pat Boone
10: Guitar Tango
- The Shadows

Valli And Seasons Début With Sherry

This was a vital month for The Four Seasons, the US vocal quartet who'd become one of the most consistently successful hit machines of the early mid-1960s. Nine years after the distinctive three-octave range of lead singer Frankie Valli was first heard on record it was finally featured on a single which received proper promotion.

Released in mid-August, *Sherry* raced up to No 1 in the US charts this month, quickly crossing the Atlantic to give the group (Valli, Bob Gaudio, Nick Massi and Tommy DeVito) a British and European hit.

Over the next four years they'd repeat the feat with the likes of *Big Girls Don't Cry*, *Walk Like A Man*, *Silence Is Golden* and *Rag Doll* to lay the foundations for a career which would make Valli one of the most popular international concert performers well into the 1990s.

Three Killed As Southern Governor Defies President

THE HARD FACE of US Southern white racism showed itself dramatically in Jackson today when Ross Barnett, the hard-line Governor of Mississippi, ordered state troopers to block the enrolment of black student James Meredith at the University of Mississippi. Confronted by 750 Federal Marshals sent in by President Kennedy, they became part of a city-wide riot in which three people died and more than 50 were reported injured.

James Meredith had been accompanied by the Federal Marshals when he arrived at the University to claim his place, which had been granted to him by Trustees of the college who had decided that the law on educational de-segregation must be obeyed. Ten days earlier, Governor Barnett's state troopers had barred his way. White segregationalists stormed the campus, and a riot was inevitable.

Proof that Mississippi whites were not prepared to surrender had come last night at a football stadium in Jackson when the 'Ole Miss' University band dressed in confederate uniforms and the all-white crowd rose to sing *Dixie*, the traditional Southern battle anthem.

Thalidomide Distributors To Fund Research

Almost four years after doctors in Britain and West Germany suggested that serious physical disabilities, including absence of limbs, had been caused by the use of the drug thalidomide, the company which marketed it in Britain decided to pay for research into its appalling side-effects.

An estimated 8000 babies were born with malformed or missing limbs after their mothers had taken thalidomide (or any one of the 50 various brand names used) as a remedy for morning sickness in the early months of pregnancy. Most of the victims came to light in Germany, where the drug was originally developed and manufactured, but it was the British distributor, the Distillers Company (Biochemicals) Ltd, which announced it would spend £250,000 on research.

OCT

Soul Star Brown Finances Own Recording

US rhythm & blues star James Brown recorded a live album at the Apollo Theatre in Harlem, New York, tonight - forced to finance it himself after his record company refused to cover the cost.

Brown, from Georgia, had approached King Records, the label which had signed him in 1956, about a project he believed would prove beneficial both to the company and his career. Although he had scored a few minor hits since joining King, he was a much greater success as a stage performer. A live album would, he said, help bridge the gap between the two.

Label executives were unenthusiastic, as Brown's previous albums had failed to reach the all-important *Billboard* LP chart. Undaunted, Brown arranged for the Apollo show to be recorded, and would be rewarded when *Live At The Apollo 1962* became his first and biggest chart success, and transformed him into one of the biggest-selling and most influential black artists of all time.

Nuclear War Averted As Kennedy Calls Khrushchev's Bluff In Cuba

THE WORLD BREATHED a collective deep sigh of relief today after a week of escalating tension between Russia and the US over Russia's Cuban missile bases offered the awful possibility of nuclear warfare between the superpowers. That appeared to have evaporated with the announcement that Russian leader Nikita Khrushchev had promised to dismantle the bases and ship the missiles back to Russia.

For his part, President John Kennedy had promised that there would be no invasion of Cuba by US forces, and that restrictions imposed on Cuba would be relaxed.

Diplomatic sources suggested that the President had outplayed his opponent in a deadly game of poker for the highest stakes, but had not attempted to press home his advantage since Khrushchev had dropped his condition that US missiles be removed from Turkey before Russian installations were withdrawn from Cuba. However, Khrushchev did complain about US aircraft violating Russian airspace over Siberia, for which Kennedy apologized.

It appeared that Khrushchev stepped back from the brink when he realized that if the situation did develop into all-out aggression, not only would much of the world be devastated, but it would be a war which Russia could not ultimately win.

While messages of congratulations for their statesmanlike wisdom flooded into the offices of both leaders from around the world, Mr Khrushchev's in-tray noticeably lacked supportive missives from Cuba's President, Fidel Castro - who had not been consulted by Moscow about the missile withdrawal - and China, known to be furious with Khrushchev for what its leadership considered a craven surrender and who promised to, 'stand by Cuba through thick and thin'.

Although Khrushchev appeared to have survived the encounter with his credibility intact, thanks to Kennedy not pressing his undoubted advantage to humiliate his opposite number, Russian hard-liners would view the Cuba step-down as an unacceptable humiliation.

Within two years they would succeed in removing Khrushchev from power, sentencing him to a disgraced retirement. John Kennedy's hard-line opponents in the US would arrange a far speedier, and more brutal, exit from the world stage in Dallas, Texas, on November 22, 1963.

UK TOP 10 SINGLES

1: Telstar
- The Tornados
2: Sheila
- Tommy Roe
3: The Loco-Motion
- Little Eva
4: It Might As Well Rain Until September
- Carole King
5: She's Not You
- Elvis Presley
6: Ramblin' Rose
- Nat 'King' Cole
7: You Don't Know Me
- Ray Charles
8: It'll Be Me
- Cliff Richard
9: What Now My Love
- Shirley Bassey
10: Venus In Blue Jeans
- Mark Wynter

OCTOBER 22

Soviet Spy Vassall Gets Heavy Sentence

WILLIAM VASSALL, a 38-year-old Admiralty clerk and former British Embassy worker in Moscow, was today found guilty of spying for Russia and sentenced by a London court to 18 years in prison.

Described during the case, which followed his arrest last month, as, 'a traitorous tool of the Russians', Vassall - the son of a clergyman - had divulged sensitive information to Russia over a six-year period, after being recruited by Russian agents during his posting to Moscow.

He had been photographed at a homosexual party and was then blackmailed into co-operating with Russian intelligence services on his return to Britain. In exchange, the court heard, Vassal received financial 'incentives' which effectively doubled his salary.

'He was entrapped by lust and thereafter cash kept him crooked,' said the prosecutor, Attorney General Sir John Hobson, who added damningly, 'He had neither the moral fibre nor the patriotism to alter his conduct.'

Indian-Chinese Fighting Intensifies

The dispute between India and China over border territory in the Himalayan region edged closer to fully-fledged war this month, forcing today's declaration of a state of emergency by the Indian Government.

Indian Prime Minister Pandit Nehru took this step after fierce fighting caused numerous casualties. Describing Chinese aggression as an, 'invasion of the whole of India, even though war has not been declared', he appealed for Indian students to volunteer for military training, noting, 'If China went unchecked, it would lead to the imposition of the law of the jungle.'

Strapped for funds to pay for arms and troops, Finance Minister Desai asked the Indian people to donate silver and gold items which could be exchanged for foreign currency to pay for military equipment.

Amnesty Born In London

A momentous day for world human rights came today in London when the birth of Amnesty International was announced.

A completely non-partisan and non-party political organization, Amnesty International dedicates itself to investigating, exposing and fighting breaches of civil liberties by governments and other bodies.

That mission would see Amnesty International pitched against regimes of all persuasions all over the world, with many political prisoners winning their freedom after they'd become the subject of successful publicity campaigns.

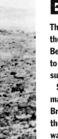

Big Times Loom For The Beatles

This month saw the start of the transformation of The Beatles from wannabe hopefuls to world-dominating superstars.

Signed to a five-year management contract with Brian Epstein on October 2, their first single, *Love Me Do,* was released by Parlophone three days later. On October 12 they returned to Merseyside, for a show at the Tower Ballroom, New Brighton, with US rocker Little Richard.

Their TV début came on October 17 when, on the Granada show *People & Places,* they performed *Love Me Do* and *Ooh My Soul* - a Little Richard song. Eleven days later The Beatles stepped onto the stage of the Liverpool Empire, their home town's biggest theatre, for the first time. This time they were in the company of Little Richard, pop star Craig Douglas, ex-Shadow Jet Harris, entertainer Kenny Lynch and British rock band Sounds Incorporated.

Although *Love Me Do* would reach no higher than No 17 in the British charts, the ball was rolling. In 1963, all their dreams would come true.

DECEMBER 15

CHARLES LAUGHTON: THE BADDIE WHO MADE GOOD

Nature dictated that Charles Laughton, the Academy Award-winning, British born character actor who died today at the age of 63, never had the face or build which allowed him to play 'easy' roles. He was always plump (not the stuff of matinée idols), with a richly expressive face which - while positively jolly and cherubic in repose - could just as easily twist into a menacing mask.

Which is why, for the first five or so years of a film career which began in England in 1927, Laughton was asked to play 'heavies' in such thriller-chillers as *The Old Dark House, The Sign Of The Cross, The Island Of Lost Souls* and the British-made movie which won him that Oscar in 1933, *The Private Life Of Henry VIII.*

His ebullient, over-the-top depiction of the infamous monarch would fix that image for Henry VIII probably for all time, just as his version of Captain William Bligh in the 1935 version of *Mutiny On The Bounty* would give those involved in later remakes the devil of a job to match, let alone top.

Laughton and his wife, Elsa Lanchester, returned to England in 1936, when he took the title role in the excellent *Rembrandt,* but it was his tragic, pathetic Quasimodo in the 1939 version of *The Hunchback Of Notre Dame* which proved that Laughton was probably one of the most gifted actors of his generation as he communicated the human behind a mass of grotesque make-up.

After a long period of so-so Hollywood films between

then and 1953 (including the probably lucrative but artistically ill-judged *Abbott And Costello Meet Captain Kidd*), Laughton redeemed himself with a last productive eight-year flurry which included *Hobson's Choice, Witness For The Prosecution, Spartacus* and a final flourish, just before he died, with *Advise And Consent.*

FEBRUARY 7

GARTH BROOKS: TAKING COUNTRY INTO THE CITY

Many country music performers had already crossed the line from success with hard-core country fans to acceptance with a much larger pop audience - Dolly Parton, Willie Nelson, Glen Campbell and Waylon Jennings spring to mind - but until Garth Brooks no-one had managed to do it so outstandingly, transforming country music into a stadium event and demolishing all the barriers the music industry likes to erect to define what is one type of music and what is another.

A Garth Brooks concert really is an event, with staging, lighting and special effects worthy of the most extravagant rock shows - huge ramped stages, rings of fire, indoor 'rainstorms', and the man himself flying on a wire high above the heads of his audience while still singing - all contributing to making him one of the most popular and successful live performers in pop music history. In 1994 his records outsold the combined sales of Michael Jackson, Madonna and Bruce Springsteen.

The son of a moderately successfully 1950s country singer, Colleen Caroll, Brooks grew up in Oklahoma, exposed to the musical tastes of older brothers and sisters,

including that of top rock acts like Kiss and Aerosmith. A graduate of Oklahoma State University (with a degree in marketing), he decided there was no reason why the excitement and extravagance of theatrical rock couldn't be married with country music to make a unique hybrid.

It would take him five years of playing bars and clubs before a recording contract was offered him, and the success of his first album - it made No 1 in the country charts, as did his second single, *If Tomorrow Never Comes* - was a sign of even better and bigger things to come.

Brooks' second album, *No Fences,* was America's No 1 country album a week after its release. His third, *Ropin' The Wind,* went one better by also topping the US pop album chart in 1991, while his fourth - *The Chase* - did the same in 1992, thanks in no small part to the fact that it was the first album in history to have in excess of five million copies ordered by fans in advance!

In 1993, Brooks smashed all previous records when all 195,000 tickets for a three-night engagement at the Texas Stadium in Dallas sold out in only five hours, while his new *In Pieces* album sold a staggering 10 million copies within a month of release. A staggering 28 million people were said to have watched his in-concert TV special *This Is Garth Brooks* when it was screened at the end of the year, and his total album sales had passed 40 million by the time 1995 dawned.

Through it all, Brooks has managed to retain the affection of his original country fans, often the first to abandon a star when he or she makes it big in the pop field. He has become a phenomenon as an entertainer, a stupendously wealthy head of a publishing and merchandizing empire, and appears to be in the position of controlling his own destiny in a way that only very few manage.

WENT

US President's Brother Becomes Senator

A third member of the Kennedy clan joined his two older brothers in Washington DC's corridors of power today when Edward Kennedy survived the scandal of his Harvard exam 'fix' to win election as Senator for the State of Massachusetts, the post President Kennedy held before moving to The White House, and headquarters of the family's formidable and all-powerful political machine.

The sons of the one-time US Ambassador to Britain, millionaire Joseph Kennedy, were already the stars of the Democratic Party. With JFK President and his brother Bobby appointed Attorney General, the arrival of another member of the Kennedy dynasty to high office gave them an unrivalled power base. Indeed, many fellow Americans now regarded them as the closest thing the US had to a royal family.

TW3's Satirical Brooms Start To Sweep

A new weekly satirical show - *That Was The Week That Was* - was screened for the first time this evening by BBC Television, and began at once to honour its producers' promise to be both topical and controversial.

Most importantly, the show had a refreshingly young image. Many of the regular cast - including host David Frost and comedy actor William Rushton - were still in their twenties and had attended either Oxford or Cambridge Universities. And although *That Was The Week That Was* (or TW3, as it soon became known to the millions who regularly tuned into the late Saturday night show), included musical items, it was the often-scurrilous sketches and demolition of the British establishment which proved that the spirit of *Beyond The Fringe* was both alive and well!

Euthanasia Acquittal For Thalidomide Doctor

The continuing tragedy of those affected by the disastrous drug thalidomide, was shown in a different light in Belgium today when a doctor who had administered a lethal injection to a deformed baby was acquitted of unlawfully practising euthanasia.

Corinne van de Put, whose mother had used thalidomide to combat morning sickness, was born without arms. Her distraught parents persuaded Dr Jacques Casters to poison Corinne soon after she was born, with an overdose of barbiturates.

Dr Casters was joined by both Corinne's parents, her aunt and her grandmother in the dock. None of the five denied the charge, and while the prosecution's case emphasized that many parents provided love and support for handicapped children, the jury's not guilty verdict was greeted with general approval in all countries with thalidomide-damaged infants.

UK TOP 10 SINGLES

1: Lovesick Blues
- Frank Ifield
2: Let's Dance
- Chris Montez
3: Telstar
- The Tornados
4: Swiss Maid
- Del Shannon
5: Venus In Blue Jeans
- Mark Wynter
6: The Loco-Motion
- Little Eva
7: Bobby's Girl
- Susan Maughan
8: Sherry
- The Four Seasons
9: Devil Woman
Marty Robbins
10: Ramblin' Rose
- Nat 'King' Cole

NOVEMBER 2

Soviets Accuse British Businessman Of Spying

GREVILLE WYNNE, a London businessman who was on an export trip to sell portable trailers for exhibitions to customers in Hungary, was arrested by Russian KGB agents on spying charges today.

The 42-year-old was taken from a park in the Hungarian capital, Budapest, after hosting a party for potential customers, and flown to Moscow in a military plane accompanied by Russian counter-intelligence agents. It was not Mr Wynne's first visit to Moscow - he had attended trade fairs there previously and was known to have many acquaintances and contacts.

Western commentators were quick to point out that Wynne's arrest had come only a matter of days after the 18 year prison sentence was passed on Russian spy William Vassall by a British court, and days before the enforced resignation of a British Government minister, Thomas Galbraith, when it was learned that he had exchanged letters with Vassal. As was customary, British Government sources were just as quick to deny that Wynne had any connection with British intelligence officers or operations.

NOVEMBER 29

Cross Channel Accord Means 'Concorde'

Long-standing disagreements between Britain and France, two countries separated by only a few miles of sea but an often uncrossable gulf of rivalry, were put aside for once today when they agreed to co-operate on the construction of a new revolutionary aircraft.

Appropriately to be known as *Concorde,* the airliner was planned as a means of travelling faster than ever before, with much of its flight at supersonic speeds. It would be over five years before the fruits of this unlikely collaboration would be publicly unveiled, however, and there would be numerous obstacles put in its way before transatlantic flights became a reality.

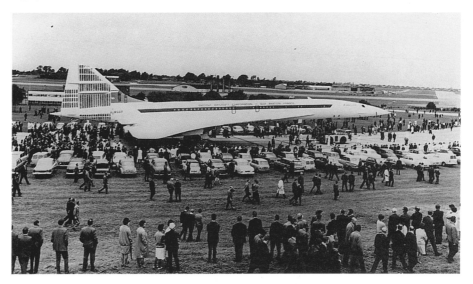

ANC's Mandela Sentenced To Five Years

IN SOUTH AFRICA, 44-year-old Nelson Mandela, the leader of the black African National Congress (ANC) civil rights organization, was sentenced to five years in prison on charges relating to his leaving the country illegally and inciting unrest.

Mandela, a gifted lawyer, had been cleverly avoiding arrest for some time after trying - but failing - to organize an illegal national strike. He was also wanted for his part in the launch of the aggressive movement known as Umkhonto we Sizwe (translated as 'Spear Of The Nation'), when he realized that his original non-violent methods could not defeat the apartheid regime.

Smuggled out of South Africa to address an African freedom conference in the Ethiopian capital, Addis Ababa, the man his followers called 'The Black Pimpernel' finally ran out of luck and was captured on his return. Today's sentence would prove only the start of Nelson Mandela's intimate knowledge of the South African prison system, but it would not signal the end of his struggle for his people's liberty from an oppressive and brutal system.

India Loses Border War With China

China offered the Indian Government a ceasefire and peace talks today when its capture of the key north-eastern centre of Bomdila gave it access to all the Assam Plains and effectively meant that India had lost the dispute over the border territories.

While officials in New Delhi tried to put a brave face on the latest developments, no one was in any real doubt that - with the Chinese able to sieze vast tracts of Indian land if it chose to - India had little option but to concede to almost any terms offered by the communists in Beijing.

Eleanor's Death Ends An Era

The US lost one of its most remarkable women - and its last link with a glorious period of its recent history - when Eleanor Roosevelt died today at the age of 78. Much more than the widow of Franklin D Roosevelt, the man who helped lead the free world to victory over Nazi Germany and Japan in World War II, the US former First Lady was very much a mover, shaker and visionary in her own right.

A New Yorker by birth, she was the niece of President Theodore Roosevelt and married her distant cousin Franklin in 1905. A dedicated social reformer and humanitarian, she wrote avidly-read newspaper columns throughout her life, and was so loathed by sections of the Republican Party who opposed her husband's nomination for the presidential candidacy in 1940 that they used the slogan 'Nor Eleanor Either' during their campaign!

Her knowledge of, and deep interest in, international affairs made her a natural choice as the first US Ambassador to the United Nations in 1946, and she served as chair of the UN Human Rights Commission from 1947 until 1951. A formidable fighter, she deserved her own place in modern US history books.

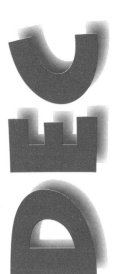

De Gaulle Says 'Non' To NATO Missile Deal

MEMBER COUNTRIES of the North Atlantic Treaty Organization today announced that a multilateral nuclear force was to be formed immediately, with Britain and France being offered US-supplied Polaris missiles.

President Kennedy and British Prime Minister Harold Macmillan broke the news at a conference in the Bahamas, after it was agreed that the US would sell the missiles to its main European allies. As a result, the joint US-British *Skybolt* rocket project was cancelled.

However, in stark contrast to last month's Anglo-French agreement to co-operate on the *Concorde* supersonic airliner project, there was no response by President de Gaulle to a personal letter from President Kennedy about the Polaris deal.

Informed speculation that de Gaulle resented Britain's 'special relationship' with the US would be confirmed dramatically on January 14, 1963 when the President not only announced France's intention of rejecting Kennedy's offer and building its own national defence system, but also blocked Britain's application for EEC membership until all trade ties with the Commonwealth were severed - a condition which he knew was unacceptable to Macmillan and the British people.

DECEMBER 12

Freed, DJ Father Of Rock'n'Roll, Faces Payola Charges

The trial of disc jockey Alan Freed (pictured), the man credited with coining the term 'rock'n'roll', began in the US today. Freed was accused of payola offences, that is, accepting bribes in return for programming particular records.

Freed was one of the first white US radio presenters to promote records by black performers, and was a hugely influential figure in the early success of performers like Chuck Berry, Little Richard, The Platters and Frankie Lymon & The Teenagers, all of whom became international stars in the mid-1950s.

Freed also appeared, as himself, in several rock'n'roll feature films, including *Rock Around The Clock* and *Don't Knock The Rock*. While few doubted that he sincerely loved rock'n'roll, there was disquiet over the fact that the songwriting credit on Chuck Berry's million-selling *Maybellene* suggested that Berry, Freed and a third person had composed the song, although it was generally accepted that Freed's name was only included as a financial inducement to ensure that the record was played regularly on his radio show.

As the music industry shuddered, and many people hurriedly covered their tracks, Freed pleaded guilty to the charges, was given a suspended prison sentence and a fine. He would die in 1965, broke and broken-hearted.

DECEMBER 6

Smog Claims 60 Lives In London

Songwriters may have found a fog-wreathed London town a fine inspiration for romantic songs, but smog - a mixture of smoke and fog - caused nothing but misery to the citizens of the British capital this week. According to official figures released today, 60 people had died in the past three days from smog-related causes. The pungent and deadly atmosphere created by domestic fires not fuelled with smokeless coal, and unfiltered industrial chimneys claimed the lives of 19 men and nine women in a single day, while hundreds of others found that ambulances were unavailable to transport them to hospitals for emergency treatment, so swamped were the emergency services.

The smog was not expected to disperse immediately, and further victims were expected. Health experts would press the government to rush through new measures to outlaw fuels which were not smoke-free.

ARRIVALS

Born this month:
6: Ben Watt, British pop singer, songwriter (Everything But The Girl)
25: Francis Dunnery, British rock musician (It Bites)

DEPARTURES

Died this month:
3: Dame Nancy Jean Gilmore, Australian poet
7: Kirsten Malfrid Flagstad, Norwegian soprano
15: Charles Laughton, British-born Academy Award-winning film actor
(see Came & Went pages)

DECEMBER 11

Wynne's Russian 'Spy Partner' Named By KGB

THE GREVILLE WYNNE case took a dramatic turn in Moscow today when a Russian intelligence officer accused of collaborating with the British businessman was arrested by the KGB and named to Western journalists.

According to the KGB, Colonel Oleg Penkovsky, who worked in Military Intelligence, had conspired with Mr Wynne for more than a year in the transmission of sensitive information relating to Russian policy in the fields of politics, science and military strength.

The 1963 trial of Wynne and the 44-year-old Penkovsky would be one of the world's most heavily publicized as Russia miled every ounce of propaganda from its revelations.

Found guilty despite their protestations of innocence, the two would receive vastly different sentences. While Penkovsky would be shot for his crime, Wynne would be sentenced to three years in prison and five in a labour camp. Released in 1964, Greville Wynne would finally admit that he had been a British spy.

DECEMBER 10

DNA Pioneers Win Nobel Prizes

Three of the scientists who first isolated, identified and described the structure of DNA - the basic biological 'building block' at the core of every living thing on earth - were awarded the Nobel Prize for Medicine in Stockholm today for work which would have a profound impact on the future of the treatment, and elimination, of many previously incurable diseases.

The three - Briton Francis Crick, US James Watson, and New Zealander Maurice Wilkins - broke the DNA code in 1953 after Crick and Watson, molecular biologists who were tackling the puzzle in Cambridge, combined their work with the separate findings of Wilkins, a biophysicist who was approaching the problem at King's College, London, with his colleague Rosalind Franklin.

The day was also a triumph for US novelist John Steinbeck, author of *The Grapes Of Wrath* and *East Of Eden*, who won the Literature Prize.

Uniquely, US chemist Linus Pauling was awarded his second Nobel Prize - the Peace Prize - in Oslo. That was in recognition of his work in the nuclear disarmament movement. He had won the Chemistry Prize in 1954 for his isolation of the cause of the killer, sickle-cell anemia.

DECEMBER 19

Nyasaland To Win Independence

Nyasaland, part of the nine-year-old Central African Federation, was today told that it could secede from the union - the first step to gaining its independence.

The decision was immediately described as 'treachery' by the Federal Prime Minister, Sir Roy Welensky, who pointed out that Britain had promised that no country would be allowed to leave the Federation unless all members agreed.

However, the strenuous opposition to federation by Nyasaland's leader, Dr Hastings Banda, meant a change of rules and Nyasaland gaining its independence in February 1963. It also inevitably meant the collapse of the Federation and, in the long term, Southern Rhodesia's decision to break with Britain completely in 1965.

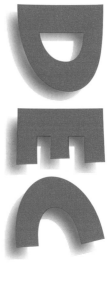

'Hot Line' Planned For Nuclear Emergencies

President Kennedy today won widespread approval when he suggested that a direct telephone link should be installed between the White House and the Kremlin to help eliminate future misunderstandings in cases of emergency.

Given the close-shave experience of the Cuban crisis, other world leaders agreed that closer relations between the two major world powers could only be an improvement on events then, when the prospect of World War III was very real. There was fervent hope on both sides of the Iron Curtain that a 'hot line' connection would help avoid tragic - and potentially deadly - confusion.

Unlike most Western horoscope systems which group astrological signs into month-long periods based on the influence of 12 constellations, the Chinese believe that those born in the same year of their calendar share common qualities with one of 12 animals - Rat, Ox, Tiger, Rabbit, Dragon, Snake, Horse, Sheep, Monkey, Rooster, Dog or Pig.

They also allocate the general attributes of five natural elements - Earth, Fire, Metal, Water, Wood - and an overall positive or negative aspect to each sign to summarize its qualities.

If you were born between February 15, 1961 and February 4, 1962, you are an Ox. As this book is devoted to the events of 1962, let's take a look at the sign which governs those born between February 5 that year and January 24, 1963 - The Year of The Tiger

THE TIGER
FEBRUARY 5, 1962 - JANUARY 24, 1963
ELEMENT: METAL ASPECT: (+)

Tigers are born leaders. They like to be in charge and the centre of attention. This comes from an innate ability to take command of any situation and run the show.

Tigers often bend the rules to suit themselves. They enjoy taking risks and have the confidence to achieve anything they want. They challenge the world alone and don't succumb to what others might think or say. They get whatever they might want or need as they have no fear of asking, learning by experience and observation.

They are not the type to take advice too kindly, should they ever need to, but this doesn't mean they're arrogant or self-promoting. On the contrary, Tigers have an inherent magnetic personality. They are friendly, talkative and interested in everyone and everything. They will always give good, honest, frank advice and possess a wide-eyed cunning innocence which is very approachable.

Tigers are compassionate, with a humanitarian approach to life and worldly problems. They will not let injustice pass by unnoticed and insist on voicing their own opinions, often leading by maybe taking the law into their own hands. The Tiger thrives on challenge.

Being adventurers gives Tigers an immense amount of energy. They can sweep everyone and everything along in their enthusiam. They are unpredictable and live for the moment, which makes them exciting.

Tigers do have their faults. They can be bad-tempered, impatient, aggressive and defensive. This comes from their unwavering conviction that what they believe is right. They are always eager to carry through their intentions and ideals, however rebellious and non-conforming they may be.

Tigers enjoy life and, as leaders, ensure their followers appreciate it as much. They are generous with all they've learned and earned, and will always ensure a global solution rather than personal gain to any problem or query.

FAMOUS TIGERS

Her Majesty the Queen

David Attenborough
Conservationist, TV wildlife guru

Richard Branson
Founder/chairman of The Virgin Group

Valéry Giscard D'Estaing
French statesman, former President of France

Sir Alec Guinness
Stage and film actor

David Owen
British politician, diplomat

Rudolf Nureyev
Russian born ballet superstar

Dame Diana Rigg
Stage and film actress

Stevie Wonder
Singer, songwriter, multi-instrumentalist, producer